The Right Plants for Dry Places

NATIVE PLANT LANDSCAPING IN CENTRAL FLORIDA

by the Publications Committee
of the
Suncoast Native Plant Society

Sheryl Bowman, Debbie Butts, Betsy Davis,
John Marsh, Ann Nord and Carl Strohmenger

A Great Outdoors Book

Great Outdoors Publishing Co.
St. Petersburg, Florida

Published by: Great Outdoors Publishing Company, Inc.
4747 28th Street North
St. Petersburg, FL 33714
(813) 525-6609

First Edition

ISBN 0-8200-0416-2

Library of Congress
Card Catalog Number
97-72213

— *PHOTO CREDITS* —

Betty Wargo: pages 16, 18, 20(t), 26, 32, 34, 36, 50(b), 56, 58, 64, 70, 82, 84, 86(t), 90, 103, 104(t), 105.

Sheryl Bowman: pages 22, 24, 30, 40, 44, 48, 68, 72, 80, 104(b).

Robin Cole/EcoStock: pages 11, 20(b), 38, 46, 52, 54, 60, 62, 66, 86(b), back cover (center and bottom)

Bob Upcavage: pages 12, 13, 14, 42, 74, 76, 88, 92

Jan Allyn: page 28, 50(t), 78, front cover, back cover (top)

— *COVER PHOTOS* —

front: Passion-flower *(Passiflora incarnata)*

back: top–gulf fritillary butterfly on goldenrod *(Solidago* spp.*)*
center–pawpaw *(Asimina reticulata)*
bottom–butterfly-weed *(Asclepias tuberosa)*

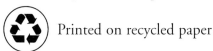 Printed on recycled paper

PRINTED IN THE UNITED STATES OF AMERICA

ACKNOWLEDGMENTS

We thank our talented photographers Jan Allyn, Sheryl Bowman, Robin Cole, Bob Upcavage, and Betty Wargo. We also thank Betsy Bicknell, Nancy Bissett, William Bissett, Matt Bradford, Joel Jackson, Billie Lofland, Brightman Logan, Ben Mercadante, Steve Riefler, Barry Wharton and Dr. Richard Wunderlin for hours of invaluable consultation. We owe Dr. Wunderlin special thanks for additional last-minute help under extreme time pressure. Finally, we are grateful to Jan Allyn for her expertise, kindness and humor in guiding us through the process of publishing our first book.

ABOUT THE FLORIDA NATIVE PLANT SOCIETY

The Florida Native Plant Society is a not-for-profit corporation whose purpose is the preservation, conservation, and restoration of the native plants and native plant communities of Florida. FNPS members throughout Florida are organized into area chapters, and the Suncoast Native Plant Society is one of those chapters. Membership meetings, field trips, plant sales and other activities are scheduled by individual chapters and usually are open to the public. For the name of the FNPS chapter nearest you, write to the Florida Native Plant Society at P. O. Box 6116, Spring **727** Hill, FL 34611, call 813-856-8202, or access fnpsbetsy@aol.com or http://www.flmnh.ufl.edu/fnps/fnps.htm. For information about the Suncoast Native Plant Society, write the Society at P. O. Box 82893, Tampa, FL 33682.

TABLE OF CONTENTS

GROUNDCOVER 73, 91,

VINES 65, 67, 79,

WILDFLOWERS 59, 61, 63, 69, 71, 75, 77, 87, 89, 93

GRASS 81, 83, 85,

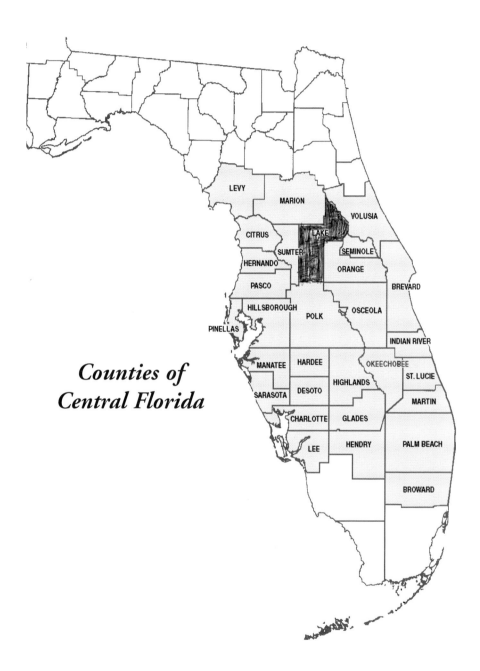

Counties of Central Florida

LEVY

MARION

VOLUSIA

CITRUS

LAKE

SUMTER

SEMINOLE

HERNANDO

ORANGE

PASCO

BREVARD

HILLSBOROUGH

OSCEOLA

PINELLAS

POLK

INDIAN RIVER

MANATEE

HARDEE

OKEECHOBEE

SARASOTA

DESOTO

HIGHLANDS

ST. LUCIE

MARTIN

CHARLOTTE

GLADES

LEE

HENDRY

PALM BEACH

BROWARD

INTRODUCTION

Why Native Plants Are Right For You

If you plant a variety of natives, your land will come alive with the lovely sights, floral fragrances, melodious bird and insect songs and varied wildlife activity of our unique central Florida heritage.

Used in suitable locations, native plants are easy and fun to grow and require exceptionally little maintenance. They have adapted over many centuries to nature's harshest conditions—heat, humidity, insects, storms, floods, freeze, frost and drought. These plants are tolerant of central Florida's dry seasons and hot, wet summers. Furthermore, native wildflowers commonly re-seed, coming back year after year on their own. Once your landscape is established, you can relax and enjoy it.

You help preserve the environment by using native plants. You conserve natural resources, such as water and fossil fuels, and also provide food and shelter for native wildlife.

What is a Florida Native Plant?

According to the *Checklist of the Vascular Plants of the Florida Suncoast* (Wunderlin *et al.*, 1995), a plant is native to Florida if it was present here in 1513, when Juan Ponce de León arrived, or if it arrived after 1513 by non-human means such as air, animal or sea drift.

What is Native Plant Landscaping?

Native plant landscaping is based on the principle of putting the right plant in the right place. Rather than first choosing your plants and then modifying the site to suit them (a process that often requires much time, effort, topsoil, fertilizer, pesticide, water and mulch), you first determine the nature of your site and then select native plants that will thrive in that location. An easy way to make your selection is to choose plants that grow in natural habitats similar to your site. Once established in the right place, your plants will require very little maintenance. Even though there are some differences between soils in the wild and urban soils that have been disturbed, many native plants, including the ones in this book, do extremely well on urban plots.

If your soil is dry, inland and in central Florida, then we wrote this book especially for you. Your soil is:

DRY if puddles disappear within a few minutes after a heavy rain,

INLAND if your property does not touch any saltwater body and does not receive salt spray in the wind and

IN CENTRAL FLORIDA if your property lies in the shaded area of the map on page 6.

① First, read "Basics of Native Plant Landscaping for Dry Central Florida Sites" starting on page 10. This section includes much information that is specific to native plant landscaping, so please read it even if you are experienced in other, more traditional, landscaping methods.

② Then use the next section, "Plant Descriptions and Photographs," starting on page 16, to select your plants. The "Quick Reference Guide" on page 94 can help you do this more quickly. If you are interested in a certain characteristic, such as a specific height at maturity or the ability to tolerate shade, you can scan the "Quick Reference Guide," find plants with that characteristic, then refer back to the plant descriptions for more detail.

③ We selected the plants in this book for ease of growing and availability. Unfortunately, we had to omit many excellent plants for lack of space. Your local chapter of the Florida Native Plant Society can recommend other suitable plants. If you cannot find a desired plant for sale, ask for it, as many nurseries will order plants upon request. See "Native Plant Sources" on page 102 for more information on this topic.

④ If you are tempted to gather from the wild rather than to purchase container-grown plants, please read "Florida Native Plant Society Policy on Transplanting Native Plants from the Wild" on page 106. You should also be aware that collecting plant material such as seeds, cuttings, leaves or whole plants from any piece of property that you do not own may violate Florida Statute 581.185, "Preservation of native flora of Florida."

⑤ For descriptions of the four major dry inland plant communities, one of which most likely was the original community of your own land, read "Dry Inland Central Florida Plant Communities" on page 103. Each plant listed in "Plant Descriptions and Photographs" naturally inhabits a number of different communities, including at least one of the four major dry inland ones.

Finally, "Resources" on pages 101–102 lists plant sources, helpful organizations and places to view native landscapes and natural habitats. The bibliography on pages 107–109 offers a varied selection of books and indicates which ones should be interesting and clear to beginning native plant gardeners.

BASICS OF NATIVE PLANT LANDSCAPING
FOR DRY CENTRAL FLORIDA SITES

Here are the basic principles and methods for planning, planting, establishment and maintenance of a native plant landscape.

PLANNING —

Native plant landscaping begins with a decision to preserve natives that are already present. The next step is to determine your soil type. If your soil meets the criteria under "Is this Book Right for You?" on page 8, most likely it will support any of the plants in this book. However, that general rule has a couple of exceptions, which we describe below in the sections on soils. Once you know your soil type you can choose plants on the basis of soil, light, size of available space and the needs of wildlife. Your plan may be as ambitious as an all-native landscape for the entire yard or as simple as a small plot of wildflowers beside the porch to attract butterflies.

PRESERVATION OF EXISTING NATIVES. If you are not sure what native plants you already have, your native plant society chapter can help with identification. If you are involved in construction of a building, protect native vegetation, including root zones, from fill, digging, scraping and damage from machinery. Ask the Cooperative Extension Service office of the county where you plan to build for information on plant protection during construction.

TYPICAL SOILS. If your soil is typical of dry inland central Florida sites, it is sandy, acid and relatively free of shells. Such soil should be suitable for any plant in this book.

However, even a typical dry site may have two kinds of areas that do not quite fit the above description. First, there may be moist spots, such as low-lying patches or places that get roof-water runoff. For such spots, use the plant descriptions in this book to find plants that tolerate moisture, or experiment with plants from moist habitats. Second, areas near limestone or concrete, such as driveways and building foundations, often have alkaline soil, which some plants cannot tolerate. The plant descriptions tell which plants to keep away from alkaline areas.

If you know you have a typical dry site—with, perhaps, some moist or alkaline spots as described above—you have enough soil information to select your plants. On the other hand, if your soil has a high content of shells or clay, the following section applies.

Coral honeysuckle makes a fine groundcover.

ATYPICAL SOILS. Occasionally, highly alkaline soil, such as soil containing numerous shells, is used for land fill. If you suspect your soil is alkaline or if you have trouble growing a number of plants from this book, have your soil tested or consult your county Cooperative Extension Service office. If you have alkaline soil, use the plant descriptions to find plants suited to such soil and consider using plants from dry coastal habitats, as these plants are adapted to alkaline conditions.

Another unusual condition may occur in soils containing large amounts of clay. Sometimes such soils show extreme dryness in the dry season and extreme wetness in the wet season. If you know your soil has a high clay content, if it fluctuates greatly between dry and wet, or if the plants from this book grow well for you in the dry season but not in the wet season, you may need to select plants that tolerate both moist and dry conditions. Plants listed as tolerant of moist soil fit this requirement. Your local chapter of the Florida Native Plant Society can provide information about other plants with wide moisture tolerance.

LIGHT. When selecting from the plant descriptions, consider sunlight as well as soil. Most dry habitat plants bloom more profusely in full sun, but some also do well in dappled shade, as noted in the individual plant descriptions.

PLANT SPACING. Because dry habitat plants need large root systems to use what water is available, it is natural for these plants to be spaced farther apart than wet habitat plants. Planting too closely may result in crowded, weedy looking plants that require thinning and pruning. The plant descriptions tell expected sizes for mature plants. Space plants far enough apart to allow room for their full growth.

*This sandhill landscape contains blazing star, Adam's needle,
pink muhlygrass, Florida paintbrush and prickly-pear cactus.*

WILDLIFE. For wildlife cover, you need a variety of plants of different
heights: groundcovers, vines, shrubs, low trees and tall trees. Include some
evergreen plants for winter shelter and bird houses or nest boxes for birds.

A varied selection of native plants provides berries, nectar and leaves
for wildlife food. In addition to cover and food, be sure to include a water
supply, such as a bird bath.

The larger the area containing desirable plants, the more likely it is to
attract wildlife. For this reason, neighbors sometimes plan wildlife gardens
together. Such planning is an exciting feature of the Florida Yards and
Neighborhoods Program, offered by your county Cooperative Extension
Service (see page 101).

For more information about attracting wildlife, see the bibliography.

PLANTING —

Now that you have selected appropriate native plants and decided
where to put them, it is time to plant. Dig your hole just deep enough
that the flat top of the root ball is level with the ground outside the hole.
It is important not to plant too deep or too shallow. After putting a plant
in the hole, fill the hole with water and then put soil back around the root
ball, firming with your hands. If the water drains so fast you cannot fill
the hole, keep watering as you add soil. Starting with water in the hole
eliminates air pockets around the roots and gives the plant a thorough ini-
tial watering.

ESTABLISHMENT —

A plant is considered established when it is able to get along without supplemental watering except in times of serious drought. Establishment of plants in a dry landscape requires frequent watering at first, followed by a tapering-off period. Depending on the plant, its size and the season, establishment can take considerable time—for some plants, more than a year. Growth will be slow until roots are established. In general, large plants take longer to establish than small ones, and all plants take longer during hot, dry seasons.

When you buy a plant, ask how long establishment takes, how frequently to water while the plant is still in the pot and what watering schedule to use after the plant is in the ground. Check new plants frequently and water them if they wilt but, outside of that, do not give water in excess of the recommended schedule. Dry habitat plants, even in containers, are quite vulnerable to overwatering.

MAINTENANCE —

Once a native plant is established in the right place, it requires very little maintenance. In this section we discuss basic maintenance issues, specifically water, fertilizer, mulch, pests and seasonal changes.

WATER. Native plants established in the proper habitat generally do not require supplemental watering. However, in times of drought, watch your plants carefully for signs of wilting, yellowing or lack of vigor, and water any struggling plants.

It is best to check for wilting in the early morning, since a plant that does not need water may still wilt in the heat of the day—and then recover

Saw palmetto is gaining in popularity as a groundcover.

13

A native wildflower garden.

overnight. It is also best to water in the early morning or in the evening, when the sun is not intense, to minimize evaporation.

2 FERTILIZER. Dry habitat plants get very little fertilizer in the wild and in fact, too much fertilizer can harm them. Furthermore, fertilizer seeps into the ground very rapidly in dry soils and may contaminate ground water. If you wish to fertilize, be sparing. Use only slow-release fertilizers and avoid high-nitrogen fertilizers, which stimulate too much top growth and not enough root development, and are costly to the environment. Fertilize in spring, fall or both, but not in summer or winter.

3 MULCH. Native plant landscaping in dry areas does not call for the large quantities of mulch used in traditional landscaping. Excess mulch eventually adds moisture-retaining organic material to the soil, making it less suitable for dry-area natives and possibly even causing the roots to rot. A thin layer of pine needles or fallen leaves is sufficient to discourage weeds and minimize dust. Take care to keep mulch from touching plant stems, because mulch holds moisture which can cause stems to rot, especially during periods of high humidity or heavy rainfall.

4 PESTS. Your landscape is part of an ecosystem, with each part dependent on every other part, so it is important to think of the effects of any action on the entire system. For example, if you use pesticides near your butterfly plants, your butterfly population will decline. Furthermore, pesticides kill beneficial insects and may cause birds to become ill or die from eating poisoned insects. When natural predators such as beneficial insects and birds die, more and more pesticides are needed to control undesirable insects, leading to ever greater expenditures of time and money and increasing threat to ground water.

14

For the health of your plants, native wildlife, your own family and pets and our water supply, avoid pesticides when possible. If you feel the need to control pests, educate yourself about pest-control methods, both natural and toxic, or consult with an expert on Integrated Pest Management (IPM).

IPM uses all kinds of insect control methods, including traps and barriers, beneficial predators, botanical insecticides, sanitation, mechanical controls and selection of appropriate plants for the site. IPM sometimes uses manufactured insecticides, but only as a last resort. In such cases, IPM favors using the insecticide that will do the job with the least danger to natural pest predators and to the environment and favors limiting insecticide applications to the affected spot. IPM strongly discourages preventive application of insecticides to healthy plants, a practice that wipes out beneficial insect populations. For further information about IPM, consult your county Cooperative Extension office.

If you avoid unnecessary insecticide applications and learn to tolerate some nibbling on leaves and fruit, the natural system will eventually reach a balance in which your plants and other creatures can live harmoniously with each other and with you, a major goal of native plant landscaping.

SEASONAL CHANGES. With native plants, you will enjoy new spring leaves, fall color changes and a seasonal progression of assorted flowers and berries. The plant descriptions tell which plants go dormant in winter, so you can save their places and watch for them to return. Since all the plants in this book are freeze-, frost- and heat-tolerant for central Florida, there is no need for special precautions based on expected temperature changes, such as covering plants before a frost. No plants are better adapted to central Florida than central Florida natives.

Hercules' club is a larval host plant for the giant swallowtail butterfly.

The spines on Hercules' club hint at the origin of its name.

COMMON NAME: Hercules' club

BOTANICAL NAME: *Zanthoxylum clava-herculis*

FAMILY: Citrus (Rutaceae)

PLANT COMMUNITIES: Dry, sandy hammocks, coastal dunes

MATURE SIZE (H X W): 15 ft. x 10 ft.

GROWTH HABIT: Small tree with a wide, spreading crown

GROWTH RATE: Moderate

DESCRIPTION: Hercules' club is a small deciduous tree armed with sharp thorns on the trunk, branches, twigs and leaves. On older plants the thorns typically slough off the trunk, leaving behind raised, conical areas. The glossy leaves alternate on the stem and are segmented into 5–19 leaflets. Each leaflet has teeth along the edges and exudes a distinct citrus smell when crushed. Small, inconspicuous, greenish-yellow flowers appear in the spring. The fruits resemble tiny green oranges, each containing up to five small, shiny black seeds.

LANDSCAPING AND MAINTENANCE: Plant as a specimen tree, along a fence row or border or to attract butterflies. This citrus family member is a larval host plant for the giant swallowtail butterfly and a nectar favorite of the great purple hairstreak butterfly.

WATER: Drought tolerant after establishment

LIGHT: Full to partial sun

SOIL: Sandy, well-drained

SALT TOLERANCE: Moderate

PROPAGATION: From seed, root cuttings. Plant on site, not in a container.

NOTES: This plant was also known as "toothache tree" by pioneers and Indians, who chewed the leaves to produce a numbing sensation in the mouth for relief of pain. The spiny trunk reminds people of the Greek legend of Hercules, who uprooted a tree to make his club.

The graceful live oak is a symbol of the Deep South.

LIVE OAK

COMMON NAME: Live oak

BOTANICAL NAME: *Quercus virginiana*

FAMILY: Oak or Beech (Fagaceae)

PLANT COMMUNITIES: Mixed hammocks, pine flatwoods, coastal areas

MATURE SIZE (H X W): 80 ft. x 100 ft.

GROWTH HABIT: A large tree with a rounded crown

GROWTH RATE: Moderate

DESCRIPTION: Live oak, considered an evergreen, drops its leaves immediately before new spring growth appears. The mature leaves are dark green, leathery, 2–5 inches long, 1–1$\frac{1}{2}$ inches wide, egg-shaped to oblong. The bark is dark and furrowed. Branches spread widely on isolated trees and may even touch the ground.

LANDSCAPING AND MAINTENANCE: Plant live oak as a specimen or shade tree. Its horizontal branches provide homes for bromeliads, orchids and ferns and are used as perching places for squirrels and birds, both of whom dine on the acorns. People appreciate the live oak for its picturesque shape and copious shade, and children find its low, spreading branches an easy climb. This "grandfather tree" is unsurpassed for large areas.

WATER: Drought tolerant after establishment; tolerates some moisture

LIGHT: Full to partial sun

SOIL: Well-drained to seasonally wet, acid to alkaline

SALT TOLERANCE: High

PROPAGATION: From acorns, grafting

NOTES: Live oaks are so named because they may live for several hundred years.

The fallen needles of longleaf pine provide free pine straw mulch.

Longleaf pine starts its life in the "grass stage", which may last for several years.

COMMON NAME: Longleaf pine

BOTANICAL NAME: *Pinus palustris*

FAMILY: Pine (Pinaceae)

PLANT COMMUNITIES: Pine flatwoods, sandhills

MATURE SIZE (H X W): 120 ft. x 35 ft.

GROWTH HABIT: Tall, upright tree with a wide crown at maturity

GROWTH RATE: Slow for 2–7 years, during which time it resembles a clump of grass, then fast

DESCRIPTION: This evergreen tree has a straight trunk and a branched, spreading crown. It is distinguished from other pines by its long green needles which grow in bundles of three. New needle growth resembles creamy white candles. The thick, reddish-brown bark forms large, shedding plates on the trunk. Winged seeds develop within very large cones.

LANDSCAPING AND MAINTENANCE: Plant as a specimen tree or for wildlife habitat. American bald eagles, red-cockaded woodpeckers, wading birds and owls use it for both perching and nesting. A variety of wildlife eats the seeds. Wide spacing will allow the crown to spread as the tree ages.

WATER: Drought tolerant after establishment, which may take up to one year after planting

LIGHT: Full sun

SOIL: Sandy, well-drained, acid

SALT TOLERANCE: Low

PROPAGATION: From seed in bare, sandy soil

NOTES: Longleaf pine is an important source of lumber and historically was used to make turpentine. Longleaf pines have been known to live up to 450 years.

The round, compact form of the myrtle oak makes it a good alternative to the larger live oak.

COMMON NAME: Myrtle oak

BOTANICAL NAME: *Quercus myrtifolia*

FAMILY: Oak or Beech (Fagaceae)

PLANT COMMUNITIES: Sand pine or oak scrubs, coastal dunes, sandhills, pine flatwoods

MATURE SIZE (H X W): 40 ft. x 8 ft.

GROWTH HABIT: Large shrub or small tree

GROWTH RATE: Moderate

DESCRIPTION: This evergreen oak may form shrubby thickets in very dry habitats or grow into a tree in moister soil. Its oval, dark-green leaves are $3/4$–2 inches long and $1/2$–1 inch wide.

LANDSCAPING AND MAINTENANCE: Plant as a barrier hedge, a small shade tree or a substitute for live oak where space is limited. Myrtle oak supplies cover, nesting and food for birds and mammals and larval food for several species of hairstreak butterflies, including the white M, the red-banded, the gray and the southern oak hairstreaks.

WATER: Drought tolerant after establishment

LIGHT: Full to partial sun

SOIL: Sandy, well-drained, acid to alkaline

SALT TOLERANCE: High

PROPAGATION: From acorns

NOTES: The acorns are important food for two species listed as threatened by the Florida Game and Fresh Water Fish Commission: the Florida scrub jay and the black bear.

Pignut hickory leaves in spring.

PIGNUT HICKORY

COMMON NAME: Pignut hickory

BOTANICAL NAME: *Carya glabra*

FAMILY: Walnut (Juglandaceae)

PLANT COMMUNITIES: Dry to mesic (moderately moist) hammocks

MATURE SIZE (H x W): 75 ft. x 30 ft.

GROWTH HABIT: Large, spreading tree

GROWTH RATE: Moderate

DESCRIPTION: Pignut hickory is a large, deciduous member of the walnut family. Its shallowly furrowed bark has a ridged, diamond pattern. The compound leaves, made up of five to seven leaflets, grow in an alternating pattern on the stem. It bears flower spikes in the spring, and the fruit is a thick-shelled nut. The leaves turn bright yellow in autumn.

LANDSCAPING AND MAINTENANCE: Plant pignut hickory as a shade or specimen tree, as a substitute for pecan, for nesting or as a food source for both people and wildlife. A long taproot makes transplanting difficult.

WATER: Drought tolerant after establishment; tolerates some moisture

LIGHT: Full to partial sun

SOIL: Sand or clay, acid to alkaline

SALT TOLERANCE: None

PROPAGATION: From seed

NOTES: The wood can be used to flavor meats during cooking.

The sand pine's crown of dense, bright green needles provide welcome shade during Florida's hot summers.

Once open, the cones of the sand pine are more round than those of other pines.

SAND PINE

COMMON NAME: Sand pine

BOTANICAL NAME: *Pinus clausa*

FAMILY: Pine (Pinaceae)

PLANT COMMUNITIES: White sand scrubs, coastal dunes

MATURE SIZE (H X W): 70 ft. x 10 ft.

GROWTH HABIT: Upright, conical tree which tends to lean over with age

GROWTH RATE: Fast

DESCRIPTION: This evergreen tree resembles Virginia pine or jack pine. It has pairs of needles approximately three inches long and reddish to gray bark. Numerous small, round cones stay on the tree while the wind disperses the seeds.

LANDSCAPING AND MAINTENANCE: Use as a specimen or a shade tree or for restoration. The cut branches make excellent indoor holiday accents.

WATER: Drought tolerant after establishment

LIGHT: Full sun

SOIL: Sandy, well-drained

SALT TOLERANCE: Moderate

PROPAGATION: From seed, grafting. Sow seed directly on site, not in a container, in pure white sand only.

NOTES: This tree dies after 80–100 years and may blow over when old. It is an indicator species that helps define the scrub plant community.

Sand post oak has an upright, slightly irregular shape.

The leaves of sand post oaks resemble those of northern white oaks.

28

SAND POST OAK

COMMON NAME: Sand post oak

BOTANICAL NAME: *Quercus margaretta*

FAMILY: Oak or Beech (Fagaceae)

PLANT COMMUNITIES: Scrubs, sandhills

MATURE SIZE (H X W): 40 ft. x 15 ft.

GROWTH HABIT: Small tree

GROWTH RATE: Slow to moderate

DESCRIPTION: The leaves, 2–5 inches long and $1^1/_2$–3 inches wide with three to five shallow lobes, are reminiscent of northern white oak leaves. Post oaks, which sometimes form thickets on sandy hills, produce large acorns every two to four years. The autumn reds, oranges, maroons and rusts of this deciduous tree are fabulous.

LANDSCAPING AND MAINTENANCE: Plant as a small to medium shade tree. The large acorns, sweeter than those of many oaks, are popular with mammals and wild turkeys.

WATER: Drought tolerant after establishment

LIGHT: Full to partial sun

SOIL: Sandy, well-drained

SALT TOLERANCE: None

PROPAGATION: From acorns

NOTES: People can make candy or meal for use in food from the acorns.

Summer haw is a small tree with graceful, arching branches.

SUMMER HAW

COMMON NAME: Summer haw

BOTANICAL NAME: *Crataegus michauxii*

FAMILY: Rose (Rosaceae)

PLANT COMMUNITIES: Hammocks, sandhills, scrubs

MATURE SIZE (H X W): 15 ft. x 15 ft.

GROWTH HABIT: Small tree or large shrub with a rounded, drooping form

GROWTH RATE: Slow

DESCRIPTION: Summer haw, a deciduous member of the rose family, blooms in the spring. Its five-petaled white to pinkish flowers are followed by fruits that resemble small apples and vary in color from yellow to red. The curving, thorny branches bear rounded or lobed leaves with toothed margins.

LANDSCAPING AND MAINTENANCE: Plant as a specimen tree, as a border hedge, in patios, under power lines and in other areas where you want a low tree. Cedar-apple rust can attack this species, so do not plant it near red cedar. Many animals and birds enjoy the fruit. The foliage provides good cover for ground-nesting birds.

WATER: Drought tolerant after establishment

LIGHT: Full to partial sun

SOIL: Dry, sandy, well-drained

SALT TOLERANCE: None

PROPAGATION: From seed, grafting. You need large quantities of seed to get a few plants.

NOTES: This species often is found in books under the name *Crataegus flava.* The fruit can be used to make jelly, which is said to have an apple-like taste.

Turkey oak leaves resemble those of northern red oaks.

Turkey oak in a sandhill plant community with blazing star and saw palmetto.

Turkey Oak

COMMON NAME: Turkey oak

BOTANICAL NAME: *Quercus laevis*

FAMILY: Oak or Beech (Fagaceae)

PLANT COMMUNITIES: Sandhills, scrubs, dry hammocks

MATURE SIZE (H X W): 40 ft. x 10 ft.

GROWTH HABIT: Tree with open, irregular branching

GROWTH RATE: Moderate

DESCRIPTION: The deciduous turkey oak grows into a medium-sized tree with dark, deeply furrowed bark. Its lobed, pointed leaves resemble the foot of a turkey, giving the plant its common name. The light green leaves are fuzzy and tinged with red when they emerge in the spring. This oak, which resembles red oaks of the northern U.S., displays rusty winter color in central Florida.

LANDSCAPING AND MAINTENANCE: Plant on the south side of a building for summer shade and winter sun. Space at least ten feet apart. Turkey oak combines well with longleaf pine, purple lovegrass, Elliott's lovegrass, lopsided indiangrass and bracken fern. The acorns, produced every two to three years, feed both birds and mammals.

WATER: Drought tolerant after establishment

LIGHT: Full to partial sun

SOIL: Sandy, well-drained, acid

SALT TOLERANCE: None

PROPAGATION: From acorns

NOTES: Turkey oak is one of the indicator species that define the sandhill plant community.

The corky branches of the winged elm provide nesting habitat.

WINGED ELM

COMMON NAME: Winged elm

BOTANICAL NAME: *Ulmus alata*

FAMILY: Elm (Ulmaceae)

PLANT COMMUNITIES: Dry to mesic (i.e., moderately moist) hammocks, dry slopes

MATURE SIZE (H X W): 40 ft. x 20 ft.

GROWTH HABIT: Tree with an open, rounded crown

GROWTH RATE: Fast

DESCRIPTION: This deciduous tree is distinguished by corky wings on its branches. As it matures, the limbs dive, dip and curve into a variety of shapes. In spring it produces tiny, bell-shaped clusters of yellowish red flowers, and in autumn the leaves turn yellow. In winter, the bare, twisting, corky branches look starkly exotic.

LANDSCAPING AND MAINTENANCE: Plant as a specimen, shade tree or street tree. It can substitute for Chinese elm and bottlebrush tree. Winged elm is extremely tolerant of hot weather. It provides nesting places for birds, as well as early seeds for squirrels and many species of songbirds.

WATER: Drought tolerant after establishment; also grows well in moist areas

LIGHT: Full to partial sun

SOIL: Moist to dry, slightly acid to alkaline

SALT TOLERANCE: None

PROPAGATION: From seed, stem cuttings, root cuttings, grafting

NOTES: People sometimes associate this tree with moist areas, but it also grows well in dry soil. Winged elm is a tree for all seasons.

The flowering spikes of Adam's needle may reach ten feet in height.

American Indians made rope from the filaments that curl off the edges of Adam's needle leaves.

ADAM'S NEEDLE

COMMON NAME: Adam's needle

BOTANICAL NAME: *Yucca filamentosa*

FAMILY: Agave (Agavaceae)

PLANT COMMUNITIES: Scrubs, sandhills, dry, open woods

MATURE SIZE (H X W): 2 ft. x 2 ft.

GROWTH HABIT: Compact shrub

GROWTH RATE: Moderate

DESCRIPTION: This shrub has stiff, sword-like leaves 12–18 inches long, with numerous threads along the leaf margins. The single flowering stalk reaches up to 10 feet in height; it is covered with 2-inch-long white flowers on short branches. After blooming, the mother plant slowly dies but is replaced by several suckering offspring.

LANDSCAPING AND MAINTENANCE: Clump several plants together or combine with evergreen shrubs, flowering shrubs such as garberia or groundcovers such as coral honeysuckle.

WATER: Drought tolerant after establishment

LIGHT: Full sun

SOIL: Sandy, well-drained

SALT TOLERANCE: High

PROPAGATION: From seed, root suckers

NOTES: The yucca moth lays eggs within the Adam's needle flower and then pollinates the plant, ensuring that seeds will be available to feed the larvae. Indians used the leaf "threads" for basketry, clothing, ropes, threads and lines. Adam's needle fiber is considered the strongest in North America (Brown, 1994). People can eat the young flowers in salads or cooked.

Bright yellow flowers cover Atlantic St. John's-wort much of the year.

ATLANTIC ST. JOHN'S-WORT

COMMON NAME: Atlantic St. John's-wort

BOTANICAL NAME: *Hypericum reductum*

FAMILY: St. John's-wort (Hypericaceae)

PLANT COMMUNITIES: Dry pine flatwoods, sandhills, scrubs

MATURE SIZE (H x W): 1¹/₂ ft. x 3 ft.

GROWTH HABIT: Mounding, prostrate shrub   *GROUND COVER*

GROWTH RATE: Slow

DESCRIPTION: Atlantic St. John's-wort is an evergreen shrub with five-petaled yellow flowers that cover most of the plant from spring to fall. The leaves are needlelike.

LANDSCAPING AND MAINTENANCE: Use as a woody groundcover for dry, sunny spots. Although this species is considered sturdier and longer-lived than other St. John's-worts (Riefler, 1991), it is intolerant of disturbances, such as foot traffic. Plant immediately upon purchase. If you must leave it in a container for a short period, water it regularly.   *NO FOOT TRAFFIC*

WATER: Drought tolerant after establishment

LIGHT: Full sun

SOIL: Sandy, well-drained

SALT TOLERANCE: None

PROPAGATION: Collect seeds late in the year and grow in 35% Canadian peat, 65% sand or perlite. Germination occurs 2–3 weeks after sowing. Transplant to a larger container after three months and to the ground after one year. Do not transplant to the ground in extremely dry seasons. This shrub is difficult to establish but, once established, easy to maintain.

NOTES: "Wort" is an old name for "plant." St. John's-worts often bear flowers on St. John's Day, June 24—hence the name. At one time, this plant was thought to protect against witches.

Coontie is an adaptable species that will thrive in full to partial sun.

COMMON NAME: Coontie

BOTANICAL NAME: *Zamia pumila*

FAMILY: Cycad (Cycadaceae)

PLANT COMMUNITIES: Hammocks, pine flatwoods, Indian middens

MATURE SIZE (H X W): 1$^1/_2$ ft. x 3 ft.

GROWTH HABIT: Mounding shrub

GROWTH RATE: Slow

DESCRIPTION: Coontie is a low, evergreen, fern-like shrub with leathery leaves. New leaves emerge from the center of the plant in growth spurts once or twice a year. Sometimes they are covered with rusty fuzz that is shed as they expand, becoming a dark, glossy green. Male and female "flowers" are produced in cone-like structures on separate plants. The female cones produce large red seeds, poisonous to people if eaten.

LANDSCAPING AND MAINTENANCE: Coontie is popular for its tropical look. It is perfect as a specimen plant, in mass plantings, in drifts with other groundcovers, around pines or tall palms or in medians.

WATER: Drought tolerant after establishment; tolerates some moisture provided drainage is good.

LIGHT: Full to partial sun

SOIL: Sandy, well-drained, acid to alkaline

SALT TOLERANCE: High

PROPAGATION: Very slow, from seed. Allow fruit to wither, then remove skin and fleshy pulp from seed before planting. An alternative method is to dry fruit in a basket or mesh bag for several months, crack with a nutcracker, then plant.

NOTES: American Indians harvested the coontie's large, woody, underground stem, removed the poisonous compounds and pounded it into flour. Settlers in south Florida manufactured starch from the stem.

Coontie belongs to one of the oldest plant families on earth, the cycads, sometimes called "dinosaurs of the plant kingdom." In south Florida, coontie leaves provide larval food for the atala butterfly.

Coral bean is noted for its magnificent red flower spikes, arrow-shaped leaves and attractive seed pods.

CORAL BEAN

COMMON NAME: Coral bean or Cherokee bean

BOTANICAL NAME: *Erythrina herbacea*

FAMILY: Pea (Fabaceae)

PLANT COMMUNITIES: Coastal, dry to mesic (i.e., moderately moist) hammocks, pine flatwoods

MATURE SIZE (H X W): 16 ft. x 4 ft. (unless pruned back by frost)

GROWTH HABIT: An upright shrub with an open growth habit

GROWTH RATE: Fast

DESCRIPTION: The most distinctive feature of this deciduous shrub is a spring display of showy red flower spikes. The brown seed pods open in summer to reveal bright scarlet seeds. The branches and stems may have spines. Each compound leaf has three arrowhead-shaped leaflets. Coral bean dies back to the ground after extreme cold but returns from the roots in spring.

LANDSCAPING AND MAINTENANCE: Plant in front of large shrubs, in coastal zones or to attract hummingbirds. Combine with pink muhlygrass, sand cordgrass, blue porterweed or tropical sage. Prune to any desired height. The large root system and long tap-root make transplanting difficult.

WATER: Drought tolerant after establishment; tolerates some moisture provided drainage is good

LIGHT: Full to partial sun

SOIL: Sandy, well-drained, acid to alkaline

SALT TOLERANCE: Moderate

PROPAGATION: From seed, stem cuttings. Nick each seed with a file (i.e., scarify it) or douse it with boiling water before planting. If kept moist, it will germinate within seven days.

NOTES: The seeds are poisonous.

Garberia produces clouds of blossoms in late fall.

COMMON NAME: Garberia

BOTANICAL NAME: *Garberia heterophylla*

FAMILY: Daisy (Asteraceae)

PLANT COMMUNITIES: Scrubs, ridges, sandhills

MATURE SIZE (H X W): 4 ft. x 6 ft.

GROWTH HABIT: Mounding shrub

GROWTH RATE: Slow

DESCRIPTION: Garberia, an evergreen member of the daisy family, has gray-green, leathery leaves and woody stems. Clusters of showy lavender blooms cover it in late fall.

LANDSCAPING AND MAINTENANCE: Plant in masses or in shrub borders. The foliage contrasts attractively with other plants. Combine with low-growing wildflowers such as beach sunflower. Garberia is an especially good nectar source for butterflies because it blooms after other flowers have finished.

WATER: Drought tolerant after establishment

LIGHT: Full sun

SOIL: Sandy, well-drained, acid

SALT TOLERANCE: Low

PROPAGATION: Plant seeds on site, not in a container, in pure white sand only. Scatter the seeds on the ground and then scratch them in with a rake.

NOTES: Garberia is listed as threatened by the Florida Department of Agriculture and Consumer Services.

Pawpaw has large fragrant white blooms.

COMBINE WITH : BLUE CURLS
BLUEBERRIES
GRASSES

COMMON NAME: Pawpaw

BOTANICAL NAME: *Asimina reticulata*

FAMILY: Custard-apple (Annonaceae)

PLANT COMMUNITIES: Pine flatwoods, pastures, sandhills

MATURE SIZE (H X W): 4 ft. x 1 ^{1}/$_2$ ft.

GROWTH HABIT: An open, spreading shrub

GROWTH RATE: Very slow

DESCRIPTION: Showy, fragrant, six-petaled white flowers appear on short, bare stems in the spring, followed by blue-green, leathery foliage. The fruit is a sweet-smelling, peanut-shaped pod containing dark brown seeds.

LANDSCAPING AND MAINTENANCE: Pawpaws are important components of many wildlife plantings and habitat recovery areas. Zebra swallow-tail butterfly larvae feed on the leaves and animals eat the fruit. Combine with blue curls, blueberries and grasses. Landscape away from concrete foundations and plant in the spring, allowing roots the entire season to establish. The large taproot prevents trans-planting.

WATER: Drought tolerant after establishment; tolerates some moisture

LIGHT: Full to partial sun

SOIL: Sandy to partially organic, acid to neutral

SALT TOLERANCE: None

PROPAGATION: From seed, root cuttings. For best results, plant on site, not in a container.

NOTES: The fruit is popular with the gopher tortoise, which is listed as a species of special concern by the Florida Game and Fresh Water Fish Commission. People also enjoy the fruit, but a few people develop allergies to it and should avoid it.

This plant resembles another pawpaw, *Asimina obovata,* which is taller (up to 12 feet) and not moisture tolerant — it requires well-drained, sandy soil.

Rusty lyonia continues to gain popularity as a landscape plant.

Rusty lyonia is known for the rusty color of its new leaves and for its urn-shaped flowers.

COMMON NAME: Rusty lyonia

BOTANICAL NAME: *Lyonia ferruginea*

FAMILY: Heath (Ericaceae)

PLANT COMMUNITIES: Scrubs, dry pine flatwoods

MATURE SIZE (H x W): 20 ft. x 5 ft.

GROWTH HABIT: Shrub or small tree with arching branches

GROWTH RATE: Slow

DESCRIPTION: The name "rusty lyonia" refers to the attractive rust-colored twigs and shoots of new growth and the rusty hairs covering the lower leaf surfaces of this dense evergreen plant. In spring, fragrant, bell-shaped, white to pink blossoms adorn shoots from the previous season.

LANDSCAPING AND MAINTENANCE: Plant in a sunny spot for a hedge, mass planting or specimen. The flowers supply nectar to a variety of insects. Prune to desired form, but do so immediately after the plant has bloomed, so shoots can develop for the next year's flowers.

WATER: Drought tolerant after establishment

LIGHT: Full to partial sun

SOIL: Sandy, well-drained, acid to slightly alkaline

SALT TOLERANCE: None

PROPAGATION: Difficult and slow, but possible, from seed

NOTES: Rusty lyonia is also called "staggerbush" because of its crooked trunks.

As a specimen or in a mass planting, saw palmetto adds variety of color and texture to the landscape.

FIREBRUSH (SHRUB)
LANTANA (GROUND COVER - SHRUB
50:ATLANTIC ST. JOHN'S - WORT
AMERICAN BEAUTY - PERRY
PINK MUHLY-GRASS

The cream-colored flowers of saw palmetto are extremely fragrant.

SAW PALMETTO

COMMON NAME: Saw palmetto

BOTANICAL NAME: *Serenoa repens*

FAMILY: Palm (Arecaceae)

PLANT COMMUNITIES: Pine flatwoods, scrubs, coastal strands

MATURE SIZE (H x W): 7 ft. x 4 ft.

GROWTH HABIT: Bushy, clump-forming shrub

GROWTH RATE: Slow

DESCRIPTION: This evergreen palm has green, hand-shaped leaves. The name "saw" refers to the stems, which are armed with curved spines. The plant produces fragrant white flowers from April to early June, and black, fleshy, one-seeded fruits in September or October. Its multiple trunks grow horizontally at or below the surface of the ground or, less commonly, upright.

LANDSCAPING AND MAINTENANCE: Saw palmetto is popular as a shrub or specimen plant, in mass plantings, beneath pine trees, under power lines, in medians and in restoration plantings. The flowers are an excellent nectar source for insects. The fruits are valuable food for insects, birds and mammals. Combine with firebush, lantana, Atlantic St. John's-wort, American beauty-berry and pink muhly-grass.

WATER: Drought tolerant after establishment; tolerates some moisture

LIGHT: Full sun to full shade

SOIL: Sandy, moist to dry, acid to alkaline

SALT TOLERANCE: Moderate

PROPAGATION: From seed, division. Both methods are slow. Divide during the warm months, March to October. You need some roots and at least two feet of trunk. Cut off the leaves, but not the leaf bud, before planting.

NOTES: A variety from Florida's east coast has silvery-blue leaves. The fat-soluble extract of saw palmetto berries is used to treat enlarged prostate. The saw palmetto is the emblem of the Florida Native Plant Society.

Scrub mint has showy flowers and aromatic foliage.

P. 58-59 BLAZING STAR (WILDFLOWER)
P. 60-61 BLUE SAGE (")
P. 68-69 FLORIDA PAINTBRUSH (")

COMMON NAME: Scrub mint

BOTANICAL NAME: *Conradina canescens*

FAMILY: Mint (Lamiaceae)

PLANT COMMUNITIES: Sand pine scrubs

MATURE SIZE (H X W): 2 ft. x 2 ft.

GROWTH HABIT: Low growing, compact shrub

GROWTH RATE: Slow

DESCRIPTION: This small, evergreen, aromatic member of the mint family has narrow, elongated, gray-green, fuzzy leaves which grow opposite each other on the stem. It bears tubular, lipped, purple-speckled flowers most of the year, with the heaviest bloom occurring in autumn.

LANDSCAPING AND MAINTENANCE: The unusual foliage is attractive in front of tall wildflowers such as blazing star, blue sage and Florida paintbrush. Scrub mint is a good nectar source for insects.

WATER: Needs water daily without fail until established; drought tolerant after establishment

LIGHT: Full sun

SOIL: Sandy, well-drained

SALT TOLERANCE: Moderate

PROPAGATION: Semi-woody cuttings taken in the spring establish readily. Also grows from seed, in pure white sand only. Sow directly into the site and rake the seed in, just deep enough so it will not blow away.

NOTES: In central Florida, scrub mint occurs naturally only in Polk and Highlands counties along the ancient geologic structure known as the Lake Wales Ridge and on the old coastal dunes in Hernando County. The leaves add a minty fragrance to potpourri.

Shiny blueberry is known for its small, glossy evergreen leaves.

The waxy blue foliage of Darrow's blueberry provides color contrast in the landscape.

The fruit of native blueberries is edible.

SHINY BLUEBERRY

COMMON NAME: Shiny blueberry

BOTANICAL NAME: *Vaccinium myrsinites*

FAMILY: Heath (Ericaceae)

PLANT COMMUNITIES: Pine flatwoods, prairies, scrubs, sandhills

MATURE SIZE (H x W): 3 ft. x 2 ft.

GROWTH HABIT: Dwarf, dense shrub

GROWTH RATE: Moderate

DESCRIPTION: This small, dense, evergreen member of the heath family has broad, glossy-green leaves. White, bell-shaped flowers with red bracts appear in spring, followed by blue-black berries. Shiny blueberry may form small colonies, spreading by stout underground stems.

LANDSCAPING AND MAINTENANCE: Plant this dwarf blueberry as a small, formal or natural hedge—it substitutes well for Japanese boxwood—or as a groundcover. It looks charming in groups around trees or palms or mixed with grasses and wildflowers.

This acid-loving plant cannot tolerate alkalinity, so keep it away from foundations, driveways or any area containing limestone or concrete. Minimize root disturbance when planting. Do not fertilize after establishment.

WATER: Drought tolerant after establishment; will not tolerate poor drainage

LIGHT: Full sun to filtered shade

SOIL: Sandy, well-drained, acid

SALT TOLERANCE: None

PROPAGATION: Seed and stem cuttings work best but both are difficult.

NOTES: Darrow's blueberry *(Vaccinium darrowii)* resembles shiny blueberry but has small, waxy, bluish-green leaves, powdery-blue fruit and no red bracts on the flowers. The waxy covering on the leaves makes this plant exceptionally drought tolerant. Landscaping and maintenance are the same as for shiny blueberry. Propagate from seed, stem cuttings or stolon (underground stem) cuttings. You can tell a stolon from a root by the stolon's leaf scales (undeveloped leaves that resemble fish scales) and by the stolon's thickness—some are almost as thick as a pencil. All three methods are difficult. The small berries of both species are delicious as a garden snack or in muffins.

If left unpruned Walter's viburnum will grow quite large and shrubby.

A multitude of white flower clusters covers Walter's viburnum in the spring.

WALTER'S VIBURNUM

COMMON NAME: Walter's viburnum

BOTANICAL NAME: *Viburnum obovatum*

FAMILY: Honeysuckle (Caprifoliaceae)

PLANT COMMUNITIES: Moist to dry hammocks, swamps, thickets, flatwoods

MATURE SIZE (H X W): 25 ft. x 10 ft.

GROWTH HABIT: A stiffly branched shrub or small tree

GROWTH RATE: Fast

DESCRIPTION: Walter's viburnum is a semi-evergreen shrub with ½- to 1-inch-long dark glossy leaves growing opposite each other on woody stems. A mass of creamy white flower clusters covers the plant in early spring, followed by flat, elliptic berries which ripen from red to black. This shrub may widen into a small thicket through growth from underground runners.

LANDSCAPING AND MAINTENANCE: Walter's viburnum makes an excellent hedge, but it can be pruned into any form, including that of a small flowering tree. Wildlife use it for cover and eat the berries.

WATER: Drought-tolerant after establishment; also grows well in moist areas

LIGHT: Full to partial sun

SOIL: Organic to sandy, slightly acid to alkaline

SALT TOLERANCE: None

PROPAGATION: From seed, stem cuttings, root cuttings. Plant seed immediately after gathering. March to June is the best time to propagate from cuttings.

NOTES: The native range covers most of Florida. Although this shrub often occurs naturally in moist woods, it also does well in dry sites, once established. The mature berries taste like raisins.

The tall spires of blazing star make a striking fall display and attract butterflies.

COMMON NAME: Blazing star

BOTANICAL NAME: *Liatris gracilis*

FAMILY: Daisy (Asteraceae)

PLANT COMMUNITIES: Dry pine flatwoods, sandhills, scrubs

MATURE SIZE (H X W): 3 ft. x $^{1}/_{2}$ ft.

GROWTH HABIT: Upright wildflower

GROWTH RATE: Moderate

DESCRIPTION: This striking perennial inhabits dry, open areas. In spring, a tuberous bulb develops at the base and sends up 12-inch elongated leaves. During late summer or early autumn it produces a 3-foot stalk with narrow, 3- to 6-inch leaves on the lower half and flower buds on the upper half. The spectacular lavender flower spike opens from the top down.

LANDSCAPING AND MAINTENANCE: Plant in masses, in a wildflower garden, in a meadow, along a roadside, or as a butterfly nectar source. Combine with the yellows of honeycomb head, goldenrod, golden aster or partridge-pea, or the white flowers of sandhill wireweed. Blazing star can last up to two weeks in a cut flower arrangement and longer as a dried flower.

WATER: Drought-tolerant after establishment

LIGHT: Full sun *FRONT YARD*

SOIL: Sandy, well-drained, slightly acid to neutral

SALT TOLERANCE: None

PROPAGATION: Collect seeds in the fall for spring planting. Scratch them into the soil but do not bury them. They need sun and light watering to germinate. This plant will reseed.

NOTES: "Blazing star" is the common name for many different species of *Liatris*. Both *Liatris gracilis* and also *Liatris tenuifolia*, two very similar plants, are excellent for dry soil but some species require moist or even wet conditions.

GROUNDCOVERS, VINES AND WILDFLOWERS

Blue sage blooms from late summer through fall.

Blue sage is the bluest of blues.

BLUE SAGE   *PERENNIAL WILDFLOWER*

COMMON NAME: Blue sage

BOTANICAL NAME: *Salvia azurea*

FAMILY: Mint (Lamiaceae)

PLANT COMMUNITIES: Pine flatwoods, sandhills, dry hammocks

MATURE SIZE (H X W): $3^{1}/_{2}$ ft. x $^{1}/_{2}$ ft.

GROWTH HABIT: Tall, thin, weakly upright <u>wildflower</u>

GROWTH RATE: Fast

DESCRIPTION: This <u>perennial</u> bears true deep-blue to nearly white, two-lipped flowers in late summer or early autumn on spikes at the ends of stems. The opposite leaves and square stems are characteristic of the mint family.

LANDSCAPING AND MAINTENANCE: Blue sage makes an excellent formal or informal border plant that blooms after most other flowers are finished. Combine with other wildflowers such as tropical sage, partridge-pea or silkgrass, with shrubs such as sandhill wireweed or garberia or with grasses.

WATER: Drought-tolerant after establishment

LIGHT: Full sun to filtered shade   *BACK YARD*

SOIL: Sandy, well-drained

SALT TOLERANCE: None

PROPAGATION: From seed, stem cuttings

NOTES: The common name "sage" evolved from the Latin botanical name "*Salvia*," meaning "safe" or "healthy," reflecting the ancient medicinal use of certain plants in this genus.

WILDFLOWERS
TROPICAL SAGE
PARTRIDGE-PEA
SILKGRASS

SHRUBS
SANDHILL WIREWEED
GARBERIA

GROUNDCOVERS, VINES AND WILDFLOWERS

Butterfly-weed is the host plant for monarch, queen and soldier butterflies.

COMBINES WELL WITH:
WILD PETUNIA
BEACH SUNFLOWER

BUTTERFLY-WEED   *PERENNIAL WILDFLOWER*

COMMON NAME: Butterfly-weed

BOTANICAL NAME: *Asclepias tuberosa*

FAMILY: Milkweed (Asclepiadaceae)

PLANT COMMUNITIES: Dry pine flatwoods, sandhills, scrubs

MATURE SIZE (H X W): 2 ft. x 3 ft.

GROWTH HABIT: Erect, slightly spreading wildflower

GROWTH RATE: Moderate

DESCRIPTION: The showy, flat-topped flower clusters of this perennial range from yellow-orange to red-orange, blooming summer through fall. Elongated leaves, varying in shape from pointed to rounded, grow in an alternating pattern on the stem. Seed pods split open when ripe, releasing dark seeds with tufts that enable them to float through the air. Butterfly-weed goes dormant each winter and grows back from tuberous roots in the spring.

LANDSCAPING AND MAINTENANCE: Combines well with wild petunia and beach sunflower. Butterfly-weed is the larval food plant for the queen, monarch, and soldier butterflies and a nectar source for a wide variety of adult butterflies.

WATER: Drought tolerant after establishment

LIGHT: Full sun   *FRONT YARD*

SOIL: Well-drained, sandy, acid to alkaline

SALT TOLERANCE: None

PROPAGATION: From seed. Close the pod with a rubber band to keep the seeds from blowing away until you are ready to collect them.

NOTES: The roots were historically used in medicines, giving rise to another common name, "pleurisy-root".

The showy yellow flowers of Carolina yellow jessamine appear in the winter when much of the landscape is still dormant.

COMMON NAME: Carolina yellow jessamine

BOTANICAL NAME: *Gelsemium sempervirens*

FAMILY: Logania (Loganiaceae)

PLANT COMMUNITIES: Thickets, hammocks, pine flatwoods

MATURE SIZE (H X W): 40 ft. x 5 ft.

GROWTH HABIT: A climbing, twining vine

GROWTH RATE: Moderate to fast

DESCRIPTION: Carolina yellow jessamine is a woody, evergreen perennial. It blooms from December to March, producing masses of yellow, five-lobed, trumpet-shaped, fragrant flowers. The smooth-edged, lance-shaped to elliptic leaves grow directly across from each other on the stems. The winged seeds are housed in long, flat capsules.

LANDSCAPING AND MAINTENANCE: Plant Carolina yellow jessamine as a groundcover or vine. As a vine it will climb deciduous trees, or cover fences, arbors, trellises or mailboxes. It adapts easily to large outdoor containers. Flowering is more profuse in full sun. Prune to prevent legginess.

WATER: Drought-tolerant after establishment; tolerates some moisture

LIGHT: Full to partial sun

SOIL: Tolerates all soils, prefers organic, well-drained

SALT TOLERANCE: None

PROPAGATION: From seed, stem cuttings, layering

NOTES: This plant contains alkaloids and should not be eaten.

GROUNDCOVERS, VINES AND WILDFLOWERS

Coral honeysuckle may serve as a trailing groundcover or climbing vine.

The tubular flowers of coral honeysuckle attract hummingbirds.

CORAL HONEYSUCKLE   VINE

COMMON NAME: Coral honeysuckle

BOTANICAL NAME: *Lonicera sempervirens*

FAMILY: Honeysuckle (Caprifoliceae)

PLANT COMMUNITIES: Thickets, hammocks

MATURE SIZE (H X W): 40 ft. x 5 ft.

GROWTH HABIT: Vine

GROWTH RATE: Slow the first year, then fast

DESCRIPTION: Coral honeysuckle is a woody, perennial vine whose leaves grow in pairs, clasping each other around the stem. The flowers appear from early spring to fall, in whorls of trumpet-shaped tubes, coral-red outside and yellow-orange inside, with scalloped or lobed rims. The fruit is red. The name "honeysuckle" comes from the sweet taste at the base of the floral tube. In south central Florida, this plant is evergreen. In north central Florida, it may lose some leaves in cold weather but normally will not die all the way back to the ground.

LANDSCAPING AND MAINTENANCE: Use coral honeysuckle as a groundcover, on slopes and roadsides, as a fence cover or on an arbor. It commonly is planted as a climbing vine to attract hummingbirds and butterflies.

WATER: Drought tolerant after establishment; tolerates moisture

LIGHT: Full to partial sun

SOIL: Adapts to a variety of soils but prefers rich, acid to neutral

SALT TOLERANCE: None

PROPAGATION: From seed, stem cuttings, layering

NOTES: This tough plant is tolerant of poor air quality, cold weather and polluted soils. It blooms best in full sun. The genus *Lonicera* was named after German naturalist Adam Lonitzer (1528–1586); the species name, *sempervirens*, means evergreen.

The fall-blooming Florida paintbrush is attractive to many species of butterflies, including this tiger swallowtail.

Florida Paintbrush *Perennial Wildflower*

COMMON NAME: Florida paintbrush

BOTANICAL NAME: *Carphephorus corymbosus*

FAMILY: Daisy (Asteraceae)

PLANT COMMUNITIES: Dry pine flatwoods, scrubs, sandhills

MATURE SIZE (H X W): 3 ft. x 1 ft.

GROWTH HABIT: Upright wildflower

GROWTH RATE: Moderate

DESCRIPTION: This perennial member of the daisy family spends most of the year as a green rosette of spatula-shaped leaves. In late summer to early autumn the plant sends up a stalk bearing a beautiful lavender head of exceptionally fragrant flowers.

LANDSCAPING AND MAINTENANCE: Plant as a nectar source in a butterfly garden, in a fall wildflower garden, or in a mass planting with yellow flowers such as goldenrod or red flowers such as tropical sage.

WATER: Drought tolerant after establishment

LIGHT: Full sun   *FRONT YARD*

SOIL: Sandy, acid

SALT TOLERANCE: None

PROPAGATION: Collect seeds in the fall. Plant in early spring, with only a light layer of soil covering the seeds.

NOTES: The green lynx spider uses the Florida paintbrush flower to raise young.

Fragrant goldenrod in a pine flatwoods plant community.

Contrary to popular belief the fall-blooming fragrant goldenrod does not trigger allergies.

FRAGRANT GOLDENROD   PERRENNIAL WILDFLOWER

COMMON NAME: Fragrant goldenrod

BOTANICAL NAME: *Solidago odora* var. *chapmanii*

FAMILY: Daisy (Asteraceae)

PLANT COMMUNITIES: Dry, open hammocks, pine flatwoods

MATURE SIZE (H X W): 4 ft. x 1 ft.

GROWTH HABIT: Upright wildflower

GROWTH RATE: Fast

DESCRIPTION: The fuzzy stems of this perennial branch several times to support small flower heads that appear only on the upper sides of the branches. These heads are composed of clusters of small, yellow, daisy-like flowers. The leaves, which alternate on the stem, contain tiny, oil-filled glands that release an anise-like odor when crushed.

LANDSCAPING AND MAINTENANCE: Plant fragrant goldenrod for yellow color from late summer through fall. Try it massed for a broad band of color. Combine in the landscape with blazing star, Florida paintbrush, blue sage or tropical sage. This species is a good butterfly nectar plant. Like many natives, it does not need mulch; however, a thin layer of pine straw or oak leaves helps it become established.

WATER: Drought tolerant after establishment

LIGHT: Full to partial sun   BACK YARD

SOIL: Sandy, well-drained

SALT TOLERANCE: None

PROPAGATION: From seed

NOTES: Goldenrod often is accused unjustly of causing allergy problems, including uncontrolled sneezing and runny sinuses. In fact, ragweed (*Ambrosia* spp.) is the culprit. Ragweed is common throughout central Florida in disturbed sites, in soils similar to those inhabited by goldenrod.

Goldenrod has a rich herbal history. It was used to treat battle wounds during the Crusades and to treat flatulence, vomiting and stomach aches in the early 1800s. It also has been used to treat ulcers and bleeding sores.

Gopher tortoises relish the fruit of gopher apple, shown above.

COMMON NAME: Gopher apple

BOTANICAL NAME: *Licania michauxii*

FAMILY: Cocoplum (Chrysobalanaceae)

PLANT COMMUNITIES: Pine flatwoods, sandhills, scrubs, coastal dunes

MATURE SIZE (H X W): 1 ft. x 8 ft.

GROWTH HABIT: Low-growing, suckering, shrubby groundcover

GROWTH RATE: Slow

DESCRIPTION: The shiny leaves of this plant arise from underground shoots. Because of gopher apple's small size and the shape and texture of its leaves, it resembles an oak seedling. Small, whitish-green flowers appear in spike-like clusters at the ends of stems in spring and summer, followed by egg-shaped fruits that are ivory-colored with a blush of reddish-purple. Gopher apple is deciduous in north Florida, semi-evergreen in central Florida and evergreen in south Florida.

LANDSCAPING AND MAINTENANCE: Use gopher apple as a woody groundcover in dry, sandy areas. It is popular for habitat plantings, as gopher tortoises and many mammals eat the fruit. Gopher apple will tolerate occasional mowing.

WATER: Drought tolerant after establishment

LIGHT: Full to partial sun   BACK YARD

SOIL: Sandy, well-drained, acid to alkaline

SALT TOLERANCE: Moderate

PROPAGATION: Plant seed two inches deep on site, not in a container, for best results.

NOTES: The species was named for the French botanist André Michaux, who traveled extensively in the United States and described this plant in the late 1700s.

Greeneyes, named for its green center, combines well with butterfly-weed and tropical sage.

WILDFLOWER:
  GREENEYES
  WILD PETUNIA (WILDFLOWER)
  TWIN FLOWER (GROUND COVER / WILDFLOWER)
  WILD PENNYROYAL (GROUND COVER)
  PURPLE LOVEGRASS (MOUNDING GRASS)

COMMON NAME: Greeneyes

BOTANICAL NAME: *Berlandiera subacaulis*

FAMILY: Daisy (Asteraceae)

PLANT COMMUNITIES: Pine flatwoods, pastures

MATURE SIZE (H X W): $1^1/_2$ ft. x 1 ft.

GROWTH HABIT: Upright wildflower

GROWTH RATE: Moderate

DESCRIPTION: This perennial gets its name from the flower, a green, disk-shaped "eye" surrounded by yellow rays. Flowering begins in spring and continues through most of the year. The lobed leaves form a basal clump. A long taproot allows this plant to survive drought, mowing and fire.

LANDSCAPING AND MAINTENANCE: Use in a mass planting or combine with other low-growing groundcovers such as wild petunia, twin-flower, wild pennyroyal or purple lovegrass.

WATER: Drought tolerant after establishment

LIGHT: Full sun   *FRONT YARD*

SOIL: Sandy, well-drained

SALT TOLERANCE: None

PROPAGATION: From seed, division. Reseeds readily. A good way to divide is to remove young plants from the edge of the colony before they develop long taproots.

NOTES: The flowers occasionally smell like chocolate.

GROUNDCOVERS, VINES AND WILDFLOWERS

P.60-61. BLUE SAGE   WILDFLOWER
P.88-89 TROPICAL SAGE WILDFLOWER
P.100   PARTRIDGE - PEA   GROUNDCOVER - WILDFLOWER

*The splendid blooming stalks of many-flowered
beardtongue are produced in the harshest of habitats.*

ROBERT VINCENT SIMS LANDSCAPE

352-589-2220

THE GARDEN REBEL

TONIC

1/3 MAGNIG EPSOM SALTS

1/3 MAGNESIUM

1/3 CHELATED IRON

DIPEL FOR CATEPILLARS

COMMON NAME: Many-flowered beardtongue

BOTANICAL NAME: *Penstemon multiflorus*

FAMILY: Saxifrage (Scrophulariaceae)

PLANT COMMUNITIES: Sandhills, dry pine flatwoods, scrubs

MATURE SIZE (H X W): 4 ft. x 1 ft.

GROWTH HABIT: Upright wildflower

GROWTH RATE: Moderate

DESCRIPTION: Many-flowered beardtongue blooms in late summer to early fall. Its upright stalk bears numerous white flowers with purplish centers, followed by capsules containing small seeds. This perennial forms a basal rosette of leaves at ground level.

LANDSCAPING AND MAINTENANCE: Use at the rear of a bed or mix with other wildflowers such as blue sage, tropical sage and partridge-pea.

WATER: Drought tolerant after establishment

LIGHT: Full to partial sun   *BACK YARD*

SOIL: Sandy, well-drained

SALT TOLERANCE: None

PROPAGATION: From seed. Reseeds readily.

NOTES: Many-flowered beardtongue works well in cut flower arrangements.

Passion-flower is a larval food for our state butterfly, the zebra longwing.

CRUCIFIXION

PASSION-FLOWER

PERENNIAL VINE

COMMON NAME: Passion-flower, maypop

BOTANICAL NAME: *Passiflora incarnata*

FAMILY: Passion-flower (Passifloraceae)

PLANT COMMUNITIES: Coastal uplands, sandhills, pine flatwoods, open fields

MATURE SIZE (H X W): 12 ft. x 5 ft.

GROWTH HABIT: Vine

GROWTH RATE: Fast

DESCRIPTION: This winding perennial vine climbs by tendrils and may produce root suckers. The matte-green, three-lobed leaves may reach 6 inches in width, and the fringed, two-toned lavender flowers average $2^1/_2$ inches in width. The large greenish-yellow fruits, known as maypops, are edible.

LANDSCAPING AND MAINTENANCE: Passion-flower is popular with butterfly gardeners, as it is the larval plant food for zebra longwing, gulf fritillary and Julia butterflies. Plant along a fence, arbor or trellis; use as a groundcover or maintain in a container. This plant may need periodic trimming as it can colonize aggressively if not controlled by caterpillars, but it does not tolerate regular mowing.

WATER: Drought tolerant after establishment, which takes longer than for most plants

LIGHT: Full sun *FRONT YARD*

SOIL: Sandy, well-drained

SALT TOLERANCE: Moderate

PROPAGATION: From seed, stem cuttings, root cuttings, layering

NOTES: The name "passion-flower" refers to the cross-shaped arrangement of flower parts, which reminds people of the crucifixion or "passion" of Christ.

ERRATA

The photograph on the cover and the one on page 78 show *Passiflora* x 'Incense,' a hybrid of two passion-flowers, the Florida native *Passiflora incarnata,* and *Passiflora cincinata.*

The long blooming period of pineywoods dropseed makes it an attractive addition to a wildflower garden.

MIX WITH: GREENEYES
TWINFLOWER
TROPICAL SAGE

PINEYWOODS DROPSEED   *PERENNIAL GRASS*

COMMON NAME: Pineywoods dropseed

BOTANICAL NAME: *Sporobolus junceus*

FAMILY: Grass (Poaceae)

PLANT COMMUNITIES: Pine flatwoods, sandhills, disturbed sites

MATURE SIZE (H X W): 2$^1/_2$ ft. x 2 ft.

GROWTH HABIT: Clumping grass

GROWTH RATE: Moderate

DESCRIPTION: Pineywoods dropseed is a perennial grass that blooms sporadically and frequently from early spring through late fall. Its reddish-purple flower spikes take the form of small pyramids. The upright leaf blades have a folded or rolled appearance.

LANDSCAPING AND MAINTENANCE: Mix with colorful wildflowers such as greeneyes, twinflower and tropical sage in open or thinly wooded areas. Use as a delicate foil for broadleaved plants. Do not combine with aggressive species that will crowd it out. Birds eat the seeds. Trim or mow to maintain a neat appearance.

WATER: Drought tolerant after establishment

LIGHT: Full sun to filtered shade   *BACK YARD*

SOIL: Sandy, well-drained

SALT TOLERANCE: None

PROPAGATION: From seed. Mow around mid-May (before the wet season) to bring about blossoms and, later, seeds. Reseeds readily.

NOTES: In many dry central Florida plant communities dropseed serves as fuel to carry rejuvenating fires.

Pink muhlygrass looks attractive in a mass planting as shown here or as an accent for wildflowers.

Pink muhlygrass provides a colorful display in the fall.

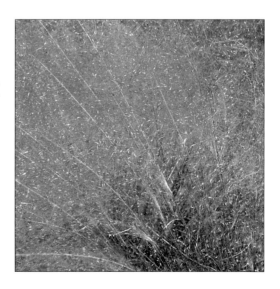

PINK MUHLYGRASS

COMMON NAME: Pink muhlygrass

BOTANICAL NAME: *Muhlenbergia capillaris*

FAMILY: Grass (Poaceae)

PLANT COMMUNITIES: Pine flatwoods, sandhills, coastal hammocks, dunes

MATURE SIZE (H X W): 3$\frac{1}{2}$ ft. x 3 ft.

GROWTH HABIT: An upright, clumping grass with an open, spreading shape

GROWTH RATE: Moderate

DESCRIPTION: Pink muhlygrass grows in clumps of wiry, rolled, gray-green leaves for most of the year. In the fall this perennial produces spectacular masses of tiny purple to pink blossoms which last six to eight weeks. After blooming, the flowers turn an attractive tan color.

LANDSCAPING AND MAINTENANCE: Plant pink muhlygrass in masses on roadside medians, as a backdrop for wildflower gardens, in coastal landscapes, as a groundcover spaced on three-foot centers and as a soil stabilizer in areas prone to erosion. Pink muhlygrass combines well with seaside goldenrod, cabbage palm and coral bean.

WATER: Drought tolerant after establishment; tolerates moisture

LIGHT: Full sun to light, shifting shade

SOIL: Sandy, acid to alkaline

SALT TOLERANCE: High

PROPAGATION: From seed. Reseeds sparsely.

NOTES: Pink muhlygrass is used by basket makers in South Carolina, who refer to it as "sweetgrass" (Yarlett, 1996).

COMBINE WITH: SEASIDE GOLDENROD
CABBAGE PALM
CORAL BEAN

Purple lovegrass makes an attractive groundcover and mixes well with wildflowers.

PURPLE LOVEGRASS

COMMON NAME: Purple lovegrass

BOTANICAL NAME: *Eragrostis spectabilis*

FAMILY: Grass (Poaceae)

PLANT COMMUNITIES: Sandhills, pine flatwoods, coastal uplands

MATURE SIZE (H X W): $1^{1}/_{2}$ ft. x $1^{1}/_{2}$ ft.

GROWTH HABIT: Mounding grass

GROWTH RATE: Fast

DESCRIPTION: This perennial grass forms a dense clump. Its flat blades may have surface hairs. In autumn it produces tiny, purple-red flowers that resemble a mist or haze when viewed from a distance.

LANDSCAPING AND MAINTENANCE: Plant as a filler or mass planting in wildflower gardens, for plant community restoration, for erosion control or for fall color on roadsides. It competes well with weeds and does not require mowing. Do not mulch during establishment.

WATER: Drought tolerant after establishment

LIGHT: Full to partial sun

SOIL: Sandy, acid to alkaline

SALT TOLERANCE: Moderate

PROPAGATION: From seed. You can spread the seeds by mowing.

NOTES: In the fall, this flowering grass graces many central Florida roadsides with a purple haze.

GROUNDCOVERS, VINES AND WILDFLOWERS

Silkgrass has daisy-like flowers.

Silkgrass, with its blue-green foliage and yellow fall blossoms, is beautiful year round.

PERENNIAL
WILDFLOWER

COMMON NAME: Silkgrass

BOTANICAL NAME: *Pityopsis graminifolia*

FAMILY: Daisy (Asteraceae)

PLANT COMMUNITIES: Dry pine flatwoods, sandhills, scrubs

MATURE SIZE (H X W): 3 ft. x 2 ft.

GROWTH HABIT: Branching, upright wildflower

GROWTH RATE: Fast

DESCRIPTION: Grass-like leaves grow in an alternating pattern on the silver-green stems of this many-branched perennial. A member of the daisy family, it produces profuse masses of small to medium, yellow, daisy-like flowers in September and October.

LANDSCAPING AND MAINTENANCE: Plant in a bed, in a mass planting or as a groundcover. Combine with other fall-blooming wildflowers such as blazing star, Florida paintbrush or blue sage. The silvery foliage creates an interesting contrast to the dark and medium greens of other plants.

WATER: Drought tolerant after establishment.

LIGHT: Full sun

SOIL: Sandy, well-drained, acid

SALT TOLERANCE: None

PROPAGATION: From seed. Mow after the seeds mature to encourage new plants.

NOTES: In spite of its name and grassy appearance, this plant is not a grass but a wildflower.

Tropical sage is easy to grow and reseeds readily.

Helianthus debilis 100
Hercules' club 16–17
hickory. *See* pignut hickory.
hog plum 100
honeysuckle. *See* coral honeysuckle.
honeycomb head 59, 100
hummingbirds 43, 67, 89
Hypericum reductum 38–39
IPM. *See* integrated pest management.
indiangrass. *See* lopsided indiangrass
insecticides 14–15
integrated pest management 15
Internet 4, 101
ironweed 100
jessamine. *See* Carolina yellow jessamine.
landscaping basics 10
lantana 51, 100
Lantana involucrata 100
Liatris
    gracilis 58–59
    tenuifolia 59
Licania michauxii 72–73
light 11
live oak 18–19, 104
longleaf pine 20–21, 33, 104, 105
Lonicera sempervirens 66–67
lopsided indiangrass 33, 100
lovegrass
    Eliott's. *See* Elliott's lovegrass.
    purple. *See* purple lovegrass.
Lyonia ferruginea 48–49
maintenance 7, 13
many-flowered beardtongue 76–77,
    104
maypop. *See* passion-flower.
mint. *See* scrub mint.
Muhlenbergia capillaris 82–83
muhlygrass. *See* pink muhlygrass.
mulch 14
myrtle oak 22–23, 103
native plants
    benefits 7
    definition 7

native plants *(continued)*
    preserving existing 10, 106
    sources for 102
    transplanting 8, 12, 106
Nolina brittoniana 100
oak
    Chapman's. *See* Chapman's oak.
    live. *See* live oak.
    myrtle. *See* myrtle oak.
    sand post. *See* sand post oak.
    turkey. *See* turkey oak.
Opuntia humifusa 100
paintbrush. *See* Florida paintbrush.
palafox 100
Palafoxia spp. 100
palm. *See* cabbage palm.
palmetto. *See* saw palmetto.
partridge-pea 59, 61, 77, 100
Passiflora incarnata 78–79
passion-flower 78–79
pawpaw 46–47
pennyroyal. *See* wild pennyroyal.
Penstemon multiflorus 76–77
Persea humilis 100
pests 7, 14–15
pignut hickory 24–25, 104
Piloblephis rigida 90–91
pine
    longleaf. *See* longleaf pine.
    sand. *See* sand pine.
pineywoods dropseed 80–81, 105
pink muhlygrass 12, 43, 51, 82–83
Pinus
    clausa 26–27
    palustris 20–21
Pityopsis graminifolia 86–87
planning 10
planting 12
plant communities 8, 103–105
plant spacing 11
pleurisy-root. *See* butterfly-weed.
Polygonella spp. 100
porterweed. *See* blue porterweed.